W9-BXY-226

HOW MONEY WORKS

FAMILY MONEY

By William Whitehead

Illustrated by Mark Beech

NORWOOD HOUSE PRESS

Chicago, Illinois

Norwood House 🏠 Press

P.O. Box 316598 · Chicago, Illinois 60631
For more information about Norwood House Press please visit our website at
www.norwoodhousepress.com or call 866-565-2900.

All images courtesy of Shutterstock except the following:
Border throughout – Eskemar; Pg 3 – (t) ukmooney (b) Kamil Macniak;
Pg 11 – federicofoto; Pg 15 – (tl) trainman; Pg 23 – plumdesign; Pg 24 – Mandy Godbehear;
Pg 25 – (t) Zurijeta (b) Jacek Chabraszewski; Pg 26/27 – shutterstock.com;
Pg 29 – (t) marikond (2nd l) Erik Lam (2nd r) Dieter H (3rd) Jagodka (b) Africa Studio;
Pg 32 – (tr)matthi (bl) Angelo Giampiccolo (br) B Brown;
Pg 33 – (l) Guy Erwood (r) Huguette Roe; Pg 34 – (t) knin (b)Bangkokhappiness;
Pg 35 – (l) falk (r) Sean Pavone Photo; Pg 37 – (tr) Art Konovalov (mr) Kazela (bl) Dariush M;
Pg 39 – (tl) Jose Ignacio Soto (tm) Eric Broder Van Dyke (tl)Goran Bogicevic (mb)Aija Lehtonen;
Pg 42 – (t) straga (m) Alistair Rennie; Pg 46 – Monkey Business Images;
Pg 47 – (t) Andrew Koturanov (2nd) Stephen Mcsweeny (3rd) Kladej (b) Creativa;
Pg 49 – (t) Phase4 Photography (ml) Jim Esposito/BLEND images/Corbis; (mr) Jouke van Keulen
(b) ~Mukesh Gupta/Reuters/Corbis; Pg 53 – shutterstock.com; Pg 54 – Vinicius Tupinamba

LIBRARY OF CONGRESS CATALOGING-IN-PUBLICATION DATA

Whitehead, William, 1942-
Family money / written by William Whitehead.
pages cm. -- (How money works)
Illustrated by Mark Beech.
Includes index.
Summary: "Presents an introduction to financial literacy and the economic factors that affect a family, such as housing, education, taxes, and income. Discusses way to manage finances through budgeting and saving. Includes index, glossary, and discussion questions"-- Provided by publisher.
ISBN 978-1-59953-717-7 (library edition : alk. paper) -- ISBN 978-1-60357-820-2 (ebook)
1. Money--Juvenile literature. 2. Income--Juvenile literature. 3. Budgets, Personal--Juvenile literature. 4. Finance, Personal--Juvenile literature. I. Beech, Mark, 1971- illustrator. II. Title.
HG221.5.W485 2015
332.024--dc23

2015003645

274N – 062015
Manufactured in the United States of America in North Mankato, Minnesota.

FAMILY MONEY

HOW FAMILIES SPEND
THEIR MONEY – AND WHY

Contents

6   Money Talk
Money is often the main topic of family conversation – after all, everyone wants a share.

8   Budgeting Right!
First you budget for the necessities. Then, if there's money to spare, the luxuries. But watch out for debt.

12   Home Sweet Home
The biggest expense a family can have is housing. But then there is also maintenance.

14   Utilities
Next you need to budget for the utilities that light and heat your home.

20   Wash and Polish
Families make a lot of mess! Who – and what – cleans up and keeps the germs at bay?

22   The Family Car
There are so many costs involved in running a car. Tax, insurance, fuel, maintenance!

24   Family Fun
Families also like to spend money on things that are fun, like vacations and pets.

30   Taxes
Governments collect taxes to pay for services that benefit everyone.

32 Services
Your local town or city uses tax funds to provide services to keep you safe, educated – and entertained.

40 Healthy Habits
Staying healthy can require spending money on things like doctor bills, hospital stays, and eating the right foods.

48 The Cost of YOU
It costs a great deal of money to keep a child – yes, YOU! You'll be amazed how much!

56 Saving for Retirement
Besides managing money that is needed now, it's important to put aside money for retirement.

58 Add It All Up!
Here's a list of items to help you tally the family expenses.

60 Let's Discuss This!

61 Additional Resources

62 Glossary

64 Index

Words that appear in red throughout the text are defined in the glossary on pages 62-63.

Money Talk

How many times have you heard your dad or mom say there's just not enough money to do this or that? They just can't afford it! The subject of money and how it's spent is always around because it's money that buys everything a family needs. And this matters to you in lots of ways.

WHY DO FAMILIES TALK about MONEY SO MUCH?

Very simply – it's money that decides the comfort and the way in which you live. Money gets talked about a lot because whether there's enough, or not enough, everyone in the family seems to need some.

Talking helps everyone understand what they can have and can't have – and how to be thankful when they CAN have something they want.

Money comes in

One of your parents, or maybe both, has a job. They work a minimum number of hours per week doing a special job in an office, a store, or some other place of work. They may even work at home.

The hours people work each week are paid at an agreed rate, and this is called a wage or salary. At the end of each week, or perhaps month, people will receive their payments. These usually go straight to their family bank account.

What jobs do parents do?

Money goes out

This money is spent on things that the family needs – the things that keep you fed, clothed, and warm – and also on the things the family wants. The money pays for the food you buy and fuel for the car, it pays for the electricity and the gas … and it buys a meal if the family wants to eat out or go to the movies, or even save for a trip or vacation.

So, where does it go exactly?

Budgeting Right!

How do parents know what they can afford and can't afford? How do they spend the money where it's needed? Most parents set a spending pattern that decides how much money will go toward buying the family essentials each week or month. This list of really important needs, and what they cost, is called a budget.

Who's in Charge?

Parents know if they spend too much on one item they will have to spend less on another. So keeping an eye on the family budget is a key job.

Who in your family is the budget "boss"?

HANDS OFF!

is there en*ugh?

What if a family doesn't have a budget?
Perhaps everyone just spends and hopes there will be
enough to go around. Does this sound like a good plan?

It may work for a time, but then comes
the unexpected. The car breaks down
or the roof starts to leak. Maybe someone
gets sick and can't go to work. This is when
the budget gets tight and everyone in the
family needs to understand what's going on.

NECESSITY?

Necessities and luxuries

Your family's monthly expenses that help keep
you clothed, warm, and fed are the necessities.
They are the key items in the budget.

Anything left over in the family fund can be
spent on things that are good to have, things
you want but don't absolutely need – items that
are known as luxuries.

LUXURY?

With*ut a budget, it's easy t* *verspend. And that means getting int* debt!

DEBTS

When you are in debt, you owe money. You may owe it to a friend or parent who doesn't care when you pay them back. But, almost certainly, when a family is in debt, it owes money to someone who DOES care!

The story of Mr. Micawber

A famous English writer, Charles Dickens, wrote a story about a man named Mr. Micawber, who spent too much.

Mr. Micawber got into so much debt he was put in prison.

But he learned his lesson and had this good advice for others ...

Annual income $1
Annual expenditure $0.99
Result HAPPINESS

Annual income $1
Annual expenditure $1.01
Result MISERY

Bank loans

If a family has a debt that it cannot pay, or wants money for a family vacation or special purchase, your parents may talk to the bank and obtain a loan. The bank will want to know that the loan can be repaid and will set a date when this must happen. Banks also charge a borrowing fee that is called interest. This is usually added to the amount of the loan and must be repaid on a regular basis.

Credit

Another way of borrowing money, where you pay much higher interest than for a bank loan, is to pay for things on a credit card. This may seem like an easy way of getting extra money, but it's still a debt, and it still has to be repaid.

Is this my problem?

Debt almost always causes worry and difficulties in a family. If you understand what is going on and why, you may be able to help by tightening your belt or just being patient for a while.

Home Sweet Home

The home you live in may have been bought by your parents, who took out a loan known as a mortgage, or it may be rented. Unless they own it outright, the cost of living in your home is almost certainly the biggest expense and budget item. On average, it amounts to about 25% of the family income.

What's a mortgage?

A mortgage is a loan from a bank or other institution to help you purchase your home. Most banks give you 25 years or so to pay off your mortgage. The money is repaid in small amounts every month.

Banks charge their normal interest. This interest fee is added to the mortgage and has to be paid back regularly as well.

What's Rent?

Homes can also be rented. Rent is a fee that's paid to the actual owner, or landlord, of the property by whoever lives in it. Rent is usually paid monthly.

The rent is agreed upon for a period of months or years under an agreement called a lease. Once the term, or period, of the lease ends, a family can renew the lease or they must move out and find another house or apartment to live in.

insurance - what is it?

Your home, all the furniture, the appliances in the kitchen, and the cars in the garage – all of these cost a lot of money. And they could all get broken or even be stolen – at any time. Fire, windstorms, flooding from heavy rainfall – these are all things that can damage your home and possessions.

Parents insure the family home and often everything in it. This means they pay a small sum of money each year to an insurance company. This company will then pay back the value of an item's repair or replacement.

upkeep ⊛R maintenance

Does the fence need a coat of paint? Does the plumber need to repair a leaky faucet, or does a wall needs fixing? These chores are necessary to keep your house and property in good order. Some of these jobs parents can do for themselves. Other projects require a professional to complete the project. Many times your parents will budget for larger projects that they cannot do themselves.

Utilities

What are they?

"Utilities" is a useful word. It describes the basic services, such as electricity, gas, or water that are delivered to our homes. It also describes the companies that supply them.

Who supplies them?

It is the utility companies that make sure the lights or the TV come on, that the oven heats up, the furnace comes on, or that water flows from the faucets. In some countries, these essential services are controlled by, even provided by, government departments. They are so important to everyone's health and safety that the government may keep an eye on how they are run and how much they charge.

What's the cost?

The companies don't give you light and heat and water for free. They charge you. It can really add up.

Huge power stations create electricity to send out across the country to your home.

network of poles
rries power through
verhead cables from
wn to town.

Dirty household water is carefully cleaned at the sewage plant. It is then pure enough to put back into the water system.

l is drilled from deep below
e surface of the sea and
ought ashore in pipes.

WHEN DO YOU PAY AND WHY?

Somewhere in your home there is a meter box for each utility. This piece of equipment is able to count how much of the service you use. Every month or so, the meter will be read by a person or automatically by computer. This reading shows how much of the service you have used and therefore how much you will then be charged. Soon after the meter is read, the household bill will arrive.

What happens if you don't pay?

The companies that supply water, gas,
r electricity expect to be paid for their services.
They may wait if you are a little late paying,
ut eventually they will warn you that they
re switching off the supply. And they will!

UTILITIES: Heating & Lighting

Electricity

Electricity provides energy to light your lightbulbs and power some of your kitchen appliances or your television. The power, which is measured in units called watts, reaches your home through cables that run from a local power-generating station.

Oil

The oil has also come a long way. It is drilled from oil fields located deep below the Earth's surface or in the seabed. Pipelines or large supertankers then carry it from country to country – sometimes half way around the world.

The electric energy comes from burning oil, natural gas, or coal, or it may have been created by nuclear energy or the power of falling water turning huge turbines. It is then carried great distances through overhead power lines over fields and mountains to your neighborhood. In towns and cities, it travels underground or through power lines strung on tall poles, and is brought to your house.

Water

Ever wonder where the water comes from and where it goes when you flush the toilet or wash the dishes in the sink? Water is supplied by a water company, or your local town.

Clean drinking water comes to your house through a water pipe connected to a larger pipe buried in the street. This is known as the water main and comes from a reservoir many miles away. This may be a lake or underground reservoir known as an aquifer.

Dirty water leaves the house from the sink, shower, or toilet and drains into a big pipe in the basement. It travels underground to an even bigger pipe under the street called a sewer.

Dirty water then flows to a sewage treatment plant which rids it of its smells and bacteria before releasing it back into the ground, river, or sea.

Gas

Many homes are heated by natural gas. This flows through pipes to your home from a huge gas cylinder, or it may be brought to your household tank by truck. Like oil, it was drilled from under the Earth's surface and brought long distances before it reaches your home.

UTILITIES: Keeping in Touch

Today, most people want to be able to talk to their family, their friends, their workplaces, and their favorite stores whenever they feel like it. They also want to be able to turn on their entertainment wherever and whenever they like. Global companies supply both the machines and the connection services – but these come at a price.

Telephone

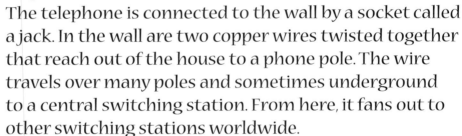

The telephone is connected to the wall by a socket called a jack. In the wall are two copper wires twisted together that reach out of the house to a phone pole. The wire travels over many poles and sometimes underground to a central switching station. From here, it fans out to other switching stations worldwide.

Cell Phones

Cell phone signals come to the phone from cellular towers spaced every few miles across the countryside. If the voice signals need to go further, they are beamed up to satellites circling the Earth and then down to a global cell tower network. Today's cell phones can do almost everything a computer can do.

ınternet

The Internet is a worldwide system of computers that are connected together. Computer users can communicate to millions of other users worldwide. The World Wide Web uses the structure of the Internet to enable access to linked documents, which are viewed using a web browser. Web pages may contain words, pictures, sounds, and videos, and users navigate between them by clicking on links.

television

Television signals may come through the same cable as the Internet. It is now possible that the screen for the computer and that for the television can be one and the same!

Letters and Packages

The postal system in many countries goes back hundreds of years. Postmen and postwomen deliver the mail each day. However, we communicate more and more with our phones and computers, leaving less mail to be delivered.

EXTINCT?

Wash and Polish

One thing a family does is make a mess! The kitchen collects spilled food and grease, and dirty pans and dishes. The bathroom collects dirt and hair around the bathtub and sink. And your bedroom? Is that clean and fresh and tidy everyday?

Cleaning wages

Almost every home needs a weekly cleaning, which means someone has to do it. Maybe your mom or dad do the cleaning, and perhaps you lend a helping hand. Or maybe your family employs someone who comes in and helps. If they do, these cleaning costs come out of the housekeeping budget.

Cleaning materials

There are special materials for every kind of cleaning job. There are sprays and liquids that dissolve grease, that kill germs, that freshen bad smells, and help remove dirt from clothes. And lots of soaps and shampoos that clean YOU!

Gadgets and machines

The cleaning equipment in a home is a big expense. Just think how many appliances your family might have that clean and iron clothes, clean floors, walls, and even clean other gadgets!

• • • • • • • • • • • • • • •

Insurance

And appliances can break! Perhaps the machinery inside breaks down or some small piece of the machine snaps off. Your family may have bought maintenance insurance, which helps pay for the repair, or even replaces the whole gadget.

Remember that insurance means paying regular, small sums of money to an organization called an insurance company to protect you if something goes wrong. The insurance company takes responsibility for the costs of any breakdown if and when that happens.

21

The Family Car

You probably often ask a parent to take you somewhere in the car. And maybe you get annoyed when they say they won't. Why should you take a bus if there's a car to be driven in? Well, the answer is that running a car is an expensive business. Putting fuel in the car is only part of the cost of running it.

BUYing it

The first and probably highest cost is the initial money used to buy or lease a car. Leasing is a kind of rental system. Most people cannot afford to buy a new car, or even a used car, outright. That means they have to borrow most of the money and pay it off in monthly amounts over a set period of time.

SMaLL aND ...

License

To drive a car you need a license. This will cost a fee. Licenses can last for a certain amount of years, then they have to be renewed.

Taxes

One of several taxes state and local governments puts on cars includes sales tax. This helps pay for the upkeep of roads, bridge and highways.

Registration

Each car has to be registered with a special office to prove ownership. This can cost more than the cost of a license in some places.

... efficient

Fuel

Most cars today are powered by gas or diesel fuel. The cost of that fuel depends on the price of a barrel of oil to the fuel companies and then the tax that governments put on it. In some countries, the tax is four times the price of the fuel. So smaller or hybrid-engine cars that run on a combination of gas and battery power, are more efficient than big gas guzzlers.

Maintenance

Even new cars need to be properly taken care of. And this means maintenance costs. Oil and filter changes, brake parts, and tires all have to be paid for. In some countries, after a number of years, a car has to undergo a safety check. Any part that's worn and could prove dangerous must be replaced. Replacement parts, as well as the cost of the check itself, have to be budgeted for.

ars piled high at a car dump.

Pollution

Cars are one of the most severe creators of pollution on our planet. They are powered by fuels that give off emissions, which are fumes that damage our health and our planet. The cars end up broken, damaged, or just plain old – and turn into huge mountains of scrap metal.

Family Fun

Parents work hard at their jobs. Kids work hard at school. And at home, there are chores to do, homework to complete, and an endless list of jobs that nobody wants to do! So free time becomes valuable.

Playing sports is a great way to spend your free time.

Of course, you may want to spend it glued to your computer or lost to the world with your headphones on, but most families try to share some activities together. And lots of these are too good to miss! Trips to amusement parks, to the movies or outdoor festivals, to restaurants, baseball games, maybe a lake – why would you want to miss out?

Fun for free

Lots of fun is free, but lots of it isn't. In many cases, the amount of fun you can enjoy depends on how much vacation or free time your family has, as well as how much money is available after paying the household expenses.

Fun for very little

A family can enjoy their leisure time without having to spend an awful lot of money. Playing games such as football in the back yard or the park just involve getting some friends together. And a bike ride into the country or through city streets can bring everyone together as well.

ree time can be spent with friends or family ...

.. or on your own!

inexpensive fun

Here are some more ways you can enjoy your leisure time without having to spend a fortune:

Have a party and invite all your friends to bring some snacks with them.

Spend a day at the beach or park. Bring your lunch!

Go to a sporting event or a concert and sit in the higher-up seats, as they are less expensive. You may be far back, but big screens can help you see the action.

VACATION TIME

Vacation time means fun for the whole family. Vacations can be taken any time, and usually last at least a week. You can take them at a resort, a beach house, a mountain lodge, or even on a cruise ship. How long you stay and how comfortable your place will be depends on what the family can afford.

Family vacations at theme parks can be a lot of fun.

If your destination means taveling to another country, then costs will rise. Most families know when they'll take a vacation well in advance. So they can budget for the cost of it by putting some money away each month. You can do the same by building your own vacation fund from pocket money or money you earn.

BUDGET ...

When companies advertise budget vacations or budget airfares, they're talking about vacations that can be bought for a cheaper price. This may mean going at different times or to different places, but you can really save some money.

Budget vacations can also mean staying nearby – or maybe renting an RV and taveling around. It can also mean taking a tour vacation. On a tour vacation, much of the stay will be organized for you, including your flight, hotel, and meals.

.. OR LUXURY

Then there are luxury vacations. These will almost certainly take you to some resort where hotels and facilities are posh. And where beach huts, entertainment, and sports activities are extra.

In the end, your vacation will depend on how much your family is willing to spend; that means setting a budget to make sure the money is available ...

... ONCE that's DONE, any vacation should be fun.

PETS

Your family might have a pet. Over half of all families in the U.S. own a pet.

Now, of course your pet may be as small as a gerbil – in which case, it will cost very little. But if it's a rather large dog, or even a horse, then the cost is going to appear equally large in the family budget.

There are about 247 million pets kept in households in the U.S.

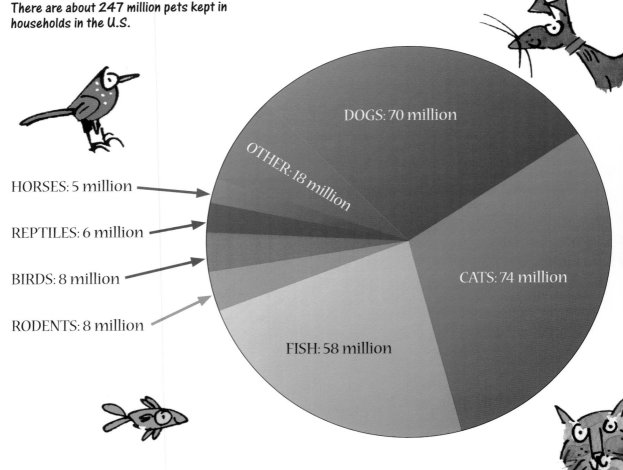

DOGS: 70 million

OTHER: 18 million

HORSES: 5 million

REPTILES: 6 million

BIRDS: 8 million

RODENTS: 8 million

CATS: 74 million

FISH: 58 million

Breakdown of pet costs:

In addition to the initial cost of adoption – and some animals cost a lot to buy – there's a whole list of expenses that the average pet owner will incur within a year.

* Toys/Presents/Treats
* Grooming
* Vet fees/Medical treatment
* Kennels
* Food

A horse can be a huge expense.

Pet Count

There are around 247 million pets living in 62% of all homes in the U.S.

* Dogs: 70 million
* Cats: 74 million
* Fish: 58 million
* Birds: 8 million

* Horses: 5 million
* Rodents: 8 million
* Reptiles: 6 million
* Other: 18 million

The Humane Society of the United States and the American Pet Products Association estimates that $22.6 billion was spent in 2014 to feed pets in the U.S.

Taxes

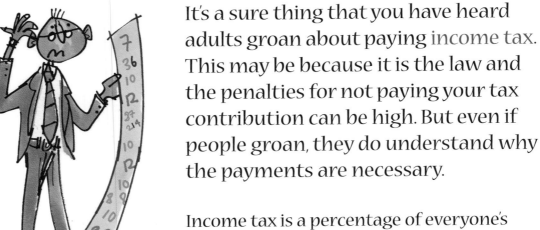

It's a sure thing that you have heard adults groan about paying income tax. This may be because it is the law and the penalties for not paying your tax contribution can be high. But even if people groan, they do understand why the payments are necessary.

Income tax is a percentage of everyone's salary that is paid to the government. Wealthy people normally pay more tax, and poorer people pay less or perhaps nothing at all. But almost everyone puts some money into the government's "kitty."

Sales tax

The government may also charge a tax on the things you buy in stores. You may have noticed this when you buy something and it costs more than it says on the label. These sales taxes may go to the state, to the county, the city, or town, and they can be as high as 10% extra added to the cost of something.

H★W are taxes spent?

The reason that every earner pays income tax is so everyone benefits. The government uses the tax it collects to pay for services everyone in the country needs – services such as healthcare, defense, education, and retirement.

Where the money goes

In the U.S., for example, the government spends about $3.8 trillion on all the things it considers important. That's an incredible amount of money!

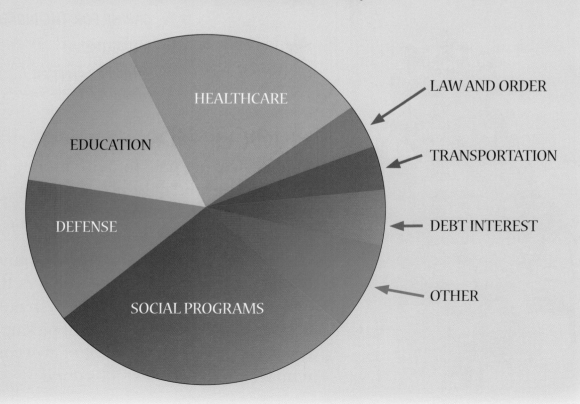

HEALTHCARE

LAW AND ORDER

EDUCATION

TRANSPORTATION

DEFENSE

DEBT INTEREST

OTHER

SOCIAL PROGRAMS

Services

In every village, town, and city, there are people who take care of our specific needs. These are things we cannot do for ourselves, such as removing the garbage, providing schools and libraries, or putting out fires. These activities are called "services" and they are carried out by men and women who mainly work in public buildings.

* GARBAGE REMOVAL & STREET CLEANING
* FIRE DEPARTMENT
* POLICE
* ROADS
* ENVIRONMENT
* PUBLIC HEALTH
* PARKS
* LIBRARIES
* DAYCARE
* ELDERLY SERVICES
* CARING FOR THE DISABLED
* MUSEUMS
* SPORTS CENTERS

A local tax

The services are paid for with money that is some kind of local tax. The tax is sometimes linked to the value of a house, or it might be based on the number of people who live there. It pays for school buildings and for teachers. It also buys the fire engines that rush out in emergencies, the trucks that pick up the garbage, and the salaries of everyone who works to get these jobs done.

Garbage removal

Every day, we toss paper and other garbage into waste baskets throughout the house. In the kitchen, bottles, cans, and food packaging are thrown into garbage cans. If we recycle, all this garbage is separated into different containers and placed for pickup. There can be quite a lot from one family alone.

Once a week, the garbage vanishes! The garbage collectors come by and carry it all away. Within hours, it's on its way to be recycled or to a huge landfill site.

Garbage must be collected before it becomes rotten or smelly and dangerous to people's health.

Thousands of tons of garbage are dumped in landfill sites.

SERVICES: Along the Road

And who takes care of the streets and roads? Every area has a local department called public works. This department fills in potholes, sweeps up the dirt, repaves the asphalt, and in colder climates, removes the snow with snow plows so the traffic can flow.

In every city, clean streets mean a healthier environment.

Over our heads, electricity, telephone, Internet, and television lines and cables are strung on poles. Pipes and sewers flow underground. The streets are the lifelines of a community, carrying essential services wherever they are needed. The public works department makes sure utility and other organizations keep these working.

Power and phone lines aren't always tidy, but they are an essential part of home and work.

Local health

Another department deals with local health concerns. Their work is to make sure we breathe in clean air, drink clean water, and use materials to build homes, businesses, and roads that are safe. This department inspects restaurant kitchens for cleanliness, and monitors the air quality for pollution.

The Local Government Purse

Daycare and schools
From an early age, you will be educated along with other children in your neighborhood.

Money must also be found for ...

Libraries
Thousands of books and other media can be borrowed or read on a comfy seat at the library.

Parks
Open spaces with trees and play areas are laid out for everyone to enjoy.

Caring for the disabled
Disabled people have special needs at school, work, and home, and the government helps.

Caring for the elderly
Elderly people cannot always take care of themselves, so senior care specialists help out.

Sports centers
Join a team or exercise on your own at the sports center.

Museums
See your favorite animals, dinosaurs, history, or art in a local museum or gallery.

SERVICES: The Fire Department

Everyone is fascinated by fire engines. It's an exciting moment when the fire alarm bell or siren starts to sound, and everyone moves to the side of the road to let the engine through.

A fire engine is sent out to house fires as well as fires in factories, offices, and stores. It carries long extension ladders to reach high roofs and holds high-pressure water hoses to quickly put out fires. These hoses connect to fire hydrants in the street, which are connected to the same water main that we get our drinking water from.

Fire engines and the firehouse ambulances also run to forest fires, automobile accidents, or someone who has fallen in their home. They may even rescue your pet cat that is stuck on the roof!

Fire work

If you want to be a firefighter, there is some tough training ahead. And you have to be smart, too, and have finished your education. But above all, you must be strong and fit. Imagine carrying an unconscious fire victim out of the third story of a burning building and down a ladder to safety!

Water is drawn from the nearest fire hydrant to the hoses.

Training

There's lots of training needed to become a firefighter. You must learn how to put out different kinds of fires. Some fires die out if water is used on the flames. Others need special liquids and foams. Firefighters learn to use special equipment such as fire hoses, ladders, extinguishers, and fire tools.

Hazards

One of the deadliest problems caused by a fire is smoke. Firefighters learn what equipment to wear and how to crawl through tight spaces, fight fires in tall buildings, and deal with hazardous materials and chemicals.

Elevated ladders can reach fires in tall buildings.

Emergency help

Firefighters may need to give emergency medical treatment on the scene. But even if this isn't necessary, firefighters must be calm and reassuring and helpful.

Several types of fire vehicles will arrive at the scene of a fire.

SERVICES: The Police

Wherever you go, you will find teams of policemen and policewomen who are there to keep order. They provide protection from thieves who rob and steal, from criminals with dangerous weapons, and indeed, from anyone who wants to hurt people or damage their property.

The police do many jobs, depending on where you live. Sometimes, special traffic police hand out tickets if you park too long or park in the wrong place. And they will stop and fine you if you are driving in a dangerous way.

But the police are there to help as well. They may help you cross the street or give you directions. They are trained to work as your friend and be there to protect you.

in Court

People who are accused of a crime must be judged in a court of law. If they are found guilty, they may be asked to pay a fine or sent to prison. The cost of this also comes from the different taxes that adults pay.

Police work

Police work means helping with everyday tasks as well as standing guard.

Whether on horseback or a fast motorcycle, the police are watchful.

Personal skills

If you want to join the police force, you will need lots of different skills. And there will be lots of exams to pass along the way! Police work can be stressful, and officers need courage and staying power!

Know it all!

The police must have basic medical knowledge to deal with emergencies, and legal knowledge to explain their actions in court. They must know how to deal with people sympathetically.

Defense

Police learn how to use firearms, defensive tactics including martial arts, how to deal with dangerous situations and people, and how not to put themselves and others in danger.

Healthy Habits

One of the most important concerns for parents is keeping the family healthy. Apart from the coughs and colds and other normal childhood diseases, parents want to make sure that any special illness is taken care of in the right way. And this kind of care can sometimes be costly.

Family Doctor

Most families have a local medical doctor or a group of doctors known as a "practice." The doctor keeps a record of all of his or her patient's illnesses. This record also includes all the patient's medications, hospital visits, and so on.

Your dentist keeps the same kinds of records about your teeth. These kinds of records mean that the care you get is based on lots of known facts.

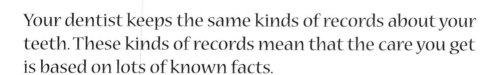

But all these records and visits and medicines cost money – money your family probably pays by way of special taxes or premiums to an insurance company.

Paying for the doctor

In many countries, the government is responsible for making sure people are kept healthy. It requires that everyone contributes something from their wages toward the cost.

Treatment

If you contribute to a health plan, you are able to see a doctor whenever you get ill. If your illness is serious, or if you have an accident, your health plan will pay for hospital treatment ... perhaps even a ride in an ambulance.

Teeth

It is important to take care of your teeth when you are young. Your dentist will tell you how to do this.

Medicines

You may need medicines to help you get better. Most of these can be supplied very cheaply or even free of charge under a healthcare plan.

FOOD ON THE TABLE

One of the biggest costs for a family is weekly food shopping. Buying basic food items is a necessity, but of course there are "luxury" foods as well. That's stuff you might like but don't really need, such as ice cream or cake.

Fresh carrots are packed with vitamins.

GROW YOUR OWN

Many years ago, when folks worked on the land, people grew their own food. Today, you can still grow food in your garden. You might grow fruit, vegetables, or even some grains. You might have chickens or goats or even a cow for milk. The food you produce will be cheaper than the food you have to buy.

Fruit is fresh but the price can vary in open-air market stalls.

But there are still costs that have to be taken into consideration. You have to invest in the seeds – and the animals – in the first place. You need tools and animal feed. Even so, growing your own food can be less costly than buying it.

42

IMPROVE YOUR health

Eating more fresh fruits and vegetables is one of the most important things you can do to stay healthy. Fruit and vegetables you've grown yourself or bought at the market look and taste good, and they have lots of vitamins.

Save money on groceries

The family food bill will shrink if you use produce from your backyard. A packet of seeds costs very little and can produce pounds of food – and you can save seeds from dead flowers and from inside the fruit and vegetables. You then dry them and plant them the following year.

Enjoy better-tasting food

Fresh food is the best food! How long has the food on your supermarket shelf been there? How long did it travel from the farm to your table? In general, foods from your garden are best!

ECO-FRIENDLY

If your house has a garden, then growing some of the food you eat is a winning way to save money – AND help the planet. You'll help reduce the use of fossil fuels and the resulting pollution that comes from the transport of fresh produce from all over the world – in planes and refrigerated trucks – to your supermarket.

ON the WINDOW SILL

Even if you don't have a big garden – or any garden for that matter – you can still grow food. Consider container gardening if you have a sunny balcony or patio, or an indoor herb garden on a windowsill. You'll be amazed at what can grow out of one pot.

AT THE STORE

Although there are open-air markets where farmers and growers sell produce they have grown themselves, most people today buy from corner stores, specialty food outlets, or giant supermarkets.

The COST OF bRANDS

Some parents will check the prices of each kind of food in the supermarket aisles. Then they will have to decide what brand to buy – the name or logo given by the manufacturer. Prices vary from brand to brand. If you recognize the name of the brand, it's usually a nationally advertised one and will cost more. The store's own brand will cost less because it's not supported by television, radio, or magazine advertising.

HOW MUCH?

Then there's the size of the container. A half gallon container of milk will cost less per quart than a one-quart container. But if the larger container isn't used up by a certain date it may spoil – so then it's not a bargain!

IS IT FRESH?

Almost all food products are marked with a date. This shows how fresh the food is and advises the best time to buy it and the expiration date before which it should be used.

EATING OUT

Mom or Dad says they don't want to cook tonight, so the family will eat out. Eating out is the most expensive way to buy food. Although costs vary from country to country, it usually costs more to eat out at restaurants, diners, delis, or fast-food joints. Most families try to include going out to eat every once in a while in their budget.

See the difference!

Made-it-at-home hamburger includes: ketchup, lettuce, tomato, bun, cheese, large hamburger
PRICE $2.50

Same hamburger at a restaurant
PRICE $6.95

Ups and downs

So what we do with our money is all about choice. Or is it?

Unfortunately, spending some of our money on shelter and food is a necessity, and therefore, we don't have many choices. In fact, most people find that most of their money is spent on necessities, so figuring out how much these will cost is essential.

Prices can go up and down and people's earnings can go up and down, so how do they do it? One way people keep tabs on what money can buy at any time is by using a measure called the "cost of living." This means just what it says – how much it costs us to live.

It's always good to check prices before you buy anything

A basket of foods

The cost of a standard basket of foodstuffs is compared over time to see how the cost changes. It can change from year to year, month to month, or even week to week, and that makes budgeting tricky.

Even the price of processed foods can vary, although producers can pay for raw foods when prices are low, but not pick them up until much later on when they are needed.

All because of the weather

The price of raw foods such as grain and coffee (usually called commodities) often depends on the weather. When there is a drought in the fields where wheat is grown, the harvest yields less wheat. There is less to sell so the price goes up. This, in turn, hikes up the price of bread and cereals.

Even the price of meat is affected. That's because with less grain to feed them, cows and other farmed animals are slaughtered earlier in their lives. There are fewer beef cattle available the following year, so the price of beef goes up along with the price of your steak and hamburger.

And it's all because of a change in the weather.

Crops may be bought when young ...

... before prices rise at harvest time.

Some crops are dried and preserved.

In a severe drought, crops fail.

47

The Cost of YOU

It's certain that parents do not see children as a COST! They love them and want to give them the very best chance to be happy. They want them to be healthy and strong and have the best opportunities to learn and develop skills. And they probably don't add up the money it takes to give all these things. But add up it does!

Let's imagine your parents will look after you from the day you are born right through to the end of your college education.

They won't spoil you, but they will cover the basic costs or necessities – like food and clothing, school, and daily travel. And they will pay for some luxuries too – after-school sports and clubs, a computer, a cell phone, pocket money and birthday presents.

In the United States, for example, your parents will be spending a whopping $245,000. If you go to college, that can add between $20,000 and $50,000 a year.

The cost of you

* Education
* Childcare and babysitting
* Food
* Clothing
* Vacations
* Hobbies and toys
* Leisure
* Pocket money
* Furniture
* Medical
* Other

Paying for childcare is a big cost for parents who work.

Developing your creative skills is an important part of your education.

Half the World

Almost half the world – over three billion people – live on less than $2.50 a day.

EDUCATION

It seems to go on forever. You get up, you go to school, you come home, you do homework. It's all about school. And sometimes you wish it would just end. But your education is probably the most important thing in your early life.

EDUCATION FOR 'FREE'

Fortunately for parents, public education in most countries is usually free. That includes elementary school, middle school, and high school. The money to build schools and hire teachers comes from the taxes adults pay either to a town, city, or state. Taxes may pay for other things such as bus transportation, text books, school sports, and special education. Not all schools are free. Private or religious-based schools generally charge a fee or tuition for attending.

EDUCATION COSTS

Parents know that without education your job opportunities become limited and the ability to earn money in the future is tougher. So what they spend will always seem worth it, and when you ask "Do I HAVE to do my homework?" – you already know the answer!

School after School

In Korea, education is supported by special tutoring. Ninety-five percent of middle school kids attend after-school tutoring agencies called hagwon. These agencies help children prepare for entry into schools with high academic standards. Korean students also attend specialized academies that teach martial arts or music. So many kids work long hours and don't get home until late.

College

Where you live often determines how much you'll have to pay for a college or university education. In most countries, taxes pay for only a small portion of the cost. Parents have to pay for most of it, or students can get a loan which must be paid off in time.

If you live away from home, this adds a further cost. You have to pay for your room and your food.

One way of lowering the cost of higher education is to earn a scholarship. This may provide you with extra funds for tuition and living. It may come from national or international scholarship funds, or from the college itself through alumni donations to the school.

YOUR CLOTHES

Are you a skimpy wardrobe person – or are your closets and drawers bulging with clothes? Or are you somewhere in between? You may be one of those people who think it's essential to have the most fashionable, and probably the most expensive shoes on the street. But the only really essential thing about clothes is to just have some.

in UniFORM

In many schools, you might spend the greater part of your time in a school uniform. This is one way to cut down on clothing expenses for young people. School uniforms may not look fashionable, but they do ensure that there's no competition to see who can dress the best and no pressure on parents to buy lots of outfits. The school uniform is the great "equalizer."

Trendy goods

Everyone knows you don't need the trendiest designer clothes to look and feel good. But this doesn't mean dressing in rags. You can get the look you want without paying top prices.

Advertisers and fashion magazines may suggest that you do, but that's their job. What you have to take into consideration is what you – or your family – can afford. The clothing portion of a parent's budget can be around 0% of the family income. That's a lot of money.

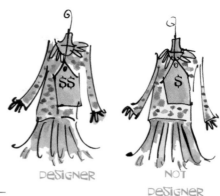

DESIGNER   NOT DESIGNER

Getting cheaper

Clothing doesn't have to be expensive. There are designer outlets that sell at discounted prices, as well as chain stores that sell inexpensive stuff.

Shop at the stores where your money buys the most for the best value.

In general, clothing today is less expensive because so much is manufactured in countries where labor costs are low.

YOUR POCKET MONEY

You probably don't get charged to live and eat in your family's home, but there are some things you need to buy for yourself. Some parents prefer to provide an allowance and that lets you decide how to manage your personal expenses.

Many parents believe it's important for you to start handling your own money at a young age. They may decide to give you a regular allowance as pocket money rather than just hand out cash whenever you ask for it.

How much pocket money you get depends on how much money the family has available to give you or how much they think you should have.

Agree on the amount

Pocket money is your first step to receiving a regular income. You may want to agree on a weekly allowance depending on how the family budget is arranged. It will also depend on how far you can trust yourself to stick to a budget. It's no good taking a weekly sum if you can't trust yourself not to blow it all in the first day!

It's possible that your pocket money comes with strings attached. These may require you to carry out certain chores around the house. You need to know EXACTLY what your family expects of you.

Your 'Earnings'

Chores may be simply helping around the kitchen or might involve just keeping your own room clean – which you should be doing anyway! They may involve caring for pets or working in the yard. Chores certainly help your family out and involve you in taking on some of the workload of the entire household.

No problem!
You're getting paid for it!

Saving for Retirement

OLD and gray

At some point, people stop working. Once this happens, their regular wage or salary payments will stop, too. However, many have probably saved a small percentage of their pay each month. And they have done this for years and years, to have money when they retire.

Some of this money is taken from their wages or salary each month and sent to the government to hold on their behalf. They may also have saved for their retirement through their employer's savings plan. Another way is putting money in a savings account and earning interest.

So ✦ - what's a retirement account?

These savings are called a retirement account. They are invested by the government and by financial companies and earn money so that the total amount grows steadily each year. This amount will finally add up to a sum that is larger than the total contributed. It will be paid back to investors after retirement.

Earning interest

When you put your money in your savings account at the bank, you expect your money to grow. This happens because the bank uses your money in its business investments and it will pay you a fee for this use. The fee is known as interest.

Interest is the profit or reward paid to the lender. Interest is interesting because anyone can do it and make their money grow a little – or sometimes a lot.

You can earn interest either as simple interest or compound interest.

Simple interest just keeps adding interest to your original amount. This is how it grows if your $1 earns interest at 10% for 5 years:

Simple Interest			
Year	Investment	Annual Rate	Ending Value
1	$1	10%	$1.10
2	$1	10%	$1.20
3	$1	10%	$1.30
4	$1	10%	$1.40
5	$1	10%	$1.50

Compound interest pays better than simple interest. The interest rate may be the same, and the time the same, but now the interest is added to the total savings AND the interest it has earned. It grows your money much faster.

Compound Interest			
Year	Investment	Annual Rate	Ending Value
1	$1	10%	$1.10
2	$1.10	10%	$1.21
3	$1.21	10%	$1.33
4	$1.33	10%	$1.46
5	$1.40	10%	$1.61

Add It All Up!

What's a budget?

A budget is an estimate of how the money that comes into the family from wages that parents and others earn is to be spent.

What comes in is called income. What goes out over this period of time is known as the "expenses."

Here is a list to add up the income that comes in and the expenses that go out for your family's budget. You can work with your family to identify expenses that you have and how much you can spend each month. There are also some tools available on the Internet. Templates for budgeting can be easily found and downloaded. From there you and your family can fill in your own numbers. You'll soon see that it pays to budget!

INCOME per month

* Wages

EXPENSES per month

* Mortgage/Rent
* Insurance
* Maintenance
* Utilities
* Cleaning
* Car loans
* Gas
* Car Repair
* Fees
* Vacations
* Pets
* Taxes
* Services
* Medical Care
* Food
* Tuition/Education
* Clothes
* Allowances
* Retirement Savings
* Other

Let's Discuss This!

CREDIT OR LOANS?

Parents might also go to the bank to get a special kind of card so they can pay for things without using cash. These are called credit or debit cards. Do you know the difference between them? Discuss which is better to use and why! Banks also give loans for things that a family needs, but cannot afford to buy outright – like a car. Can you think of other things your family might need a loan for?

SMaller bills?

There are many ways you can help to reduce costs in the family budget. Think about what costs there are around the house on a typical day – electricity, gas, water, heating, travel expenses, food shopping, clothes, etc. What can you do to reduce the bills? A few starter clues – turn off the lights when you don't need them, walk instead of taking the bus. Discuss other things you can do.

Budgeting Time

Of the expenses discussed in this book, what expenses does your family have? Does your family have additional expenses not discussed here? Discuss with a parent the items that are in your family budget and develop plans for staying on budget or earning extra income.

Additional Resources

B★★ks

Mooney, Carla. *Understanding Credit*. Minneapolis, Minnesota: Lerner Publishing Group, 2015.

Randolph, Ryan P. *How to Make a Budget*. New York, New York: Powerkids Press, 2014.

Thompson, Helen. *Banking Math*. Broomall, Pennsylvania: Mason Crest, 2014.

• •

Websites

MoneyandStuff
www.moneyandstuff.info/budgetworksheet.htm
Download budget worksheets for kids, teens, and parents. Includes tips on saving and getting credit.

The Mint
www.mint.org
A website for children and teens that includes activities and tips for earning, saving, spending, and sharing money.

Glossary

allowance
(see pocket money)

appliances
Mechanical gadgets, such as washing machines and refrigerators, that perform household tasks.

aquifer
A type of underground water reservoir.

bank account
A person's agreement with a bank to hold their money.

bill
A statement issued by a supplier to a customer requesting payment for work or supplies.

brand
A mark or name on a manufacturer's products that is easily recognized.

budget
An agreed sum to be spent.

commodities
The name given to essential products such as grains and metals that are bought and sold in large quantities.

cost of living
The price of basic home expenses that can be compared from time to time.

credit card
A card that lets you borrow money to buy goods.

debt
Borrowed money to be repaid.

essentials
Basic costs of a household. Also known as necessities.

expiration date
The date printed on certain foods before which they should be eaten.

fossil fuels
Fuels such as coal and oil that are found in the Earth.

garbage
The waste household products that are collected and destroyed or recycled.

government
The group of people elected to run a country or locality on behalf of its people.

hagwon
A private tutoring school in Korea.

healthcare
A government-run program that makes sure all people receive some form of medical care.

income
Another name for earnings.

income tax
A tax paid to the government by people who earn a certain amount.

interest
A percentage sum added to borrowed or invested money.

insurance
Small sums of money paid out to cover the possible larger costs of damage or loss to property.

invest
To place money in an
income-producing
opportunity.

lease
An agreement to occupy
a home for a fixed period
and fixed rental cost.

license
A permission given in
exchange for a payment.

luxuries
Purchases that are
wanted but not needed.

meter box
A gadget that counts
the amount of power or
water supplied to a home.

mortgage
A loan to house buyers
that is repaid over time.

pet
An animal that you have
at home for pleasure and
companionship.

pocket money
Money paid to a child for
personal expenditures.

pollution
The damage caused to
the environment by
humans.

prices
The cost of buying
something.

public works
Construction activities
undertaken by a
government on behalf of
communities.

recycle
The use of waste to make
new products.

rent
A fee you pay to live in or
use a space that belongs
to someone else.

retirement account
A repayment made
to retired people by
the government or a
company from funds
previously invested over
time.

salary
Money earned on a
regular basis in
exchange for work.

services
Activities such as
education and policing
paid for by local
governments.

sewer
Waste water and solid
products from homes
travel through these.

tax
A percentage of a family's
income or purchases
collected by governments
to provide services.

wage
Money earned on an
hourly basis in
exchange for work.

Index

advertising – 45
afford (verb) – 6, 8, 53, 60
allowance – 54, 55, 59, 60, 62
ambulance – 36, 41
appliances – 13, 16, 21, 62
aquifer – 17, 62
art gallery – 35
bank account – 7, 62
bargain – 45
bill – 7, 15, 43, 60, 62
brand – 45, 62
budget – 8, 9, 12, 13, 20, 23, 26, 27, 28, 46, 47, 53, 55, 58, 60, 62
cable – 15, 16, 19
car – 7, 9, 13, 22, 23, 59, 60
cell phone – 18
chore – 13, 24, 55, 60
cleaning – 20, 21, 32, 59
clothes – 20, 21, 52, 53, 59, 60
commodities – 47, 62
cost of living – 12, 46, 62
credit – 11, 60
credit card – 11, 60, 62
debt – 10, 11, 31, 62
defense – 31, 39
dentist – 40, 41
diesel – 23
disabled – 32, 35
doctor – 40, 41
earnings – 46, 55, 62
education – 31, 37, 48, 49, 50, 51, 59, 53
electricity – 7, 14, 15, 16, 34, 60
essentials – 8, 62
expenses – 9, 24, 29, 52, 54, 58, 59, 60, 62
expiration date – 45, 62
fire – 13, 32, 36, 37, 39
fire hydrant – 36 –
food – 7, 20, 29, 33, 42, 43, 44, 45, 46, 47, 48, 49, 51, 59, 60, 62

fossil fuel – 44, 62
fuel – 7, 22, 23, 44, 62
garbage – 32, 33, 62
garden – 42, 43, 44
gas – 7, 14, 15, 16, 17, 23, 60
government – 14, 23, 30, 31, 35, 41, 56, 62, 63
hagwon – 51, 62
health/healthcare – 14, 23, 31, 32, 33, 34, 40, 41, 43, 48, 62
hospital – 40, 41
housekeeping – 20
income – 10, 12, 30, 31, 53, 55, 58, 59, 62
income tax – 30, 31, 62
interest – 11, 12, 31, 57, 62
insurance – 13, 21, 40, 59
Internet – 19, 34, 58
investment – 57
job – 7, 8 , 13, 20, 24, 32, 38, 50, 53
landfill – 33
landlord – 12, 63
lease – 12, 22, 63
leisure – 25, 49
library – 35
license – 22, 63
loan – 11, 12, 51, 59, 60, 63
local tax – 32
luxury/ies – 9, 27, 42, 48, 60, 63
mail – 19
main (water) – 17, 36
market – 42, 43, 44, 45
medicine – 40, 41
meter – 15, 63
mortgage – 12, 59, 63
museum – 32, 35
nuclear energy – 16
park – 24, 25, 26, 32, 35, 38
pet – 28, 29, 36, 55, 59
pocket money – 26, 48, 49, 54, 55, 60, 62, 63

police – 32, 38, 39
pollution – 23, 34, 44, 63
power line – 16
power station – 15
price – 18, 23, 27, 45, 46, 47, 53, 62, 63
processed food – 47
public works – 34, 63
rent – 12, 22, 59, 63
reservoir – 17, 62
restaurant – 24, 34, 46
salary – 7, 30, 56, 63
scholarship – 51
school – 24, 32, 35, 37, 48, 49, 50, 51, 52, 62
school uniform – 48, 52
services – 14, 15, 18, 31, 32, 34, 36, 59, 63
sewage – 15, 17
shop – 42, 53, 60
simple interest – 57
sport – 24, 25, 27, 32, 35, 48, 50
supermarket – 43, 44, 45
switching station – 18
tax – 22, 23, 30, 31, 32, 38, 40, 50, 51, 59, 62, 63
telephone – 18, 34
television – 16, 19, 34, 45
traffic police – 38
turbine – 16
tutoring – 51, 62
university – 51
utilities – 14, 16, 18, 59
vet – 29
wage – 7, 20, 41, 56, 58, 59, 63
water – 14, 15, 16, 17, 34, 36, 37, 60, 62, 6
work – 7, 9, 13, 24, 32, 34, 35, 37, 38, 39, 42, 46, 49, 51, 55, 56, 57, 58, 62, 63
workplace – 18
world wide web – 19